TRAVEL
THE
WORLD

SHOP AVAILABLE TO TICKET HOLDERS ONLY

Welcome to...
Cadbury
Cadbury
WORLD
DUNEDIN NZ

contemporary
lounge
BALLANTYNES

Re:START
SUPPORTED BY ASB
3:WISEMEN
SHOES
BOOTS
HERE
NOW

MIMCO
MIMCO
Crafted Coffee Company
Taste Our Coffee, Understand Our Craft

RECEPTION
HOURS
8am -
Closes from 7pm
WARNING
THIS PROPERTY IS UNDER
CONSTANT ELECTRONIC
SURVEILLANCE!
SORRY
Closed due to
22 February earthquake
DO NOT KNOW WHEN
we are reopening
SORRY
KIA KAHA.

FIRE

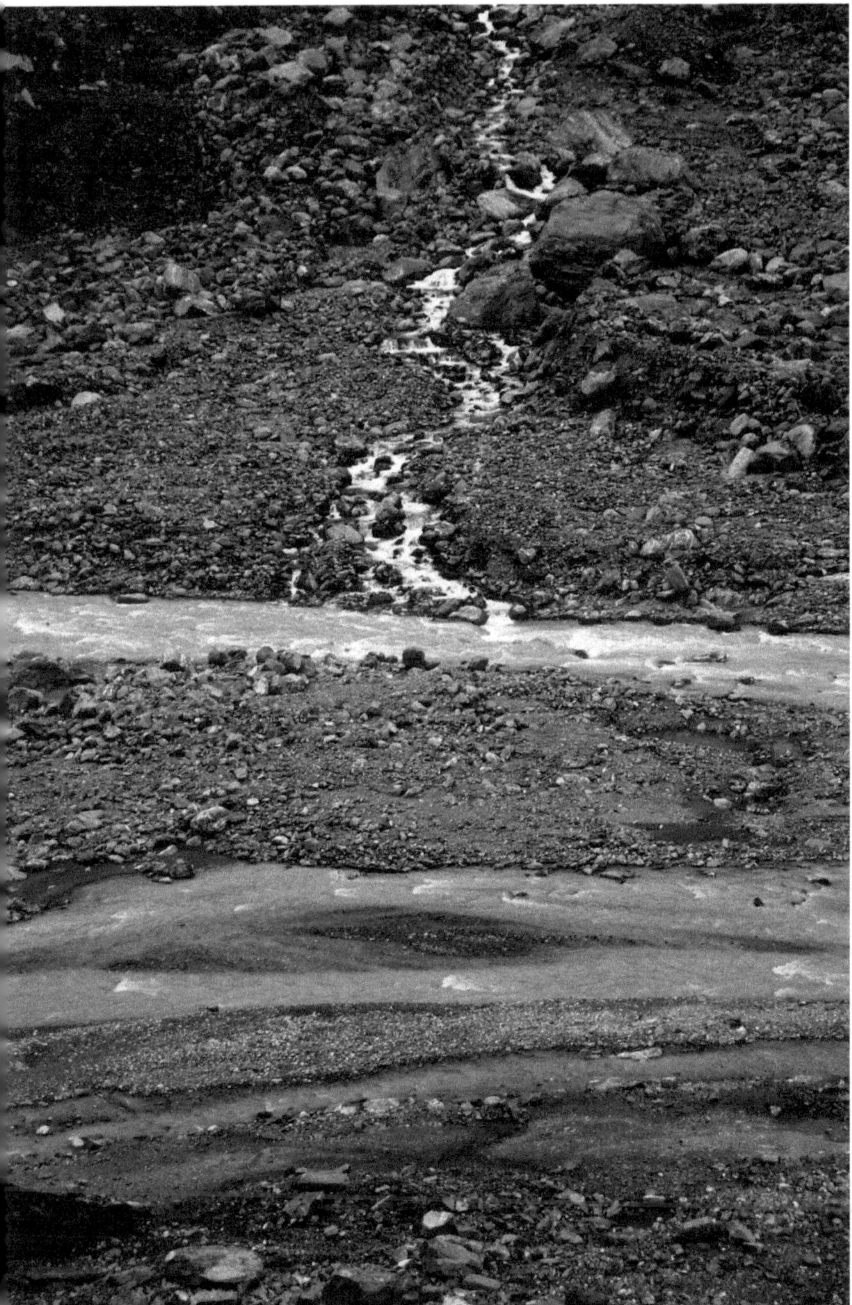

SPA UNITS
Mt. Cook View
MOTEL
INSPECTION INVITED

NATURES WONDERS
NATURES WONDERS

CPSIA information can be obtained
at www.ICGtesting.com
Printed in the USA
BVHW051128110319
542318BV00022B/1623/P

9 780368 381430